NORTHFIELD BRANCH
847-446-5990

D1267338

DRAWING
Your Pets

BY **ABBY COLICH**   ILLUSTRATED BY **STEFANO AZZALIN**

CAPSTONE PRESS
a capstone imprint

Snap Books are published by Capstone Press, a Capstone imprint
1710 Roe Crest Drive, North Mankato, Minnesota 56003
www.capstonepub.com

Library of Congress Cataloging-in-Publication Data
Colich, Abby, author.
 Drawing your pets / Written by Abby Colich ; Illustrated by Stefano Azzalin.
   pages cm. — (Drawing amazing animals)
 ISBN 978-1-4914-2134-5 (library binding)
Summary: "Gives readers easy instructions on how to draw different animals kept as pets"—
Provided by publisher.
1. Animals in art—Juvenile literature. 2. Drawing—Technique—Juvenile literature. I. Azzalin,
Stefano, illustrator. II. Title.
 NC783.8.P48C65 2015
 743.6—dc23
                    2014033158

Credits
Juliette Peters, designer
Aruna Rangarajan, cover designer
Kathy McColley, production specialist

Photo Credits
Design elements by Shutterstock

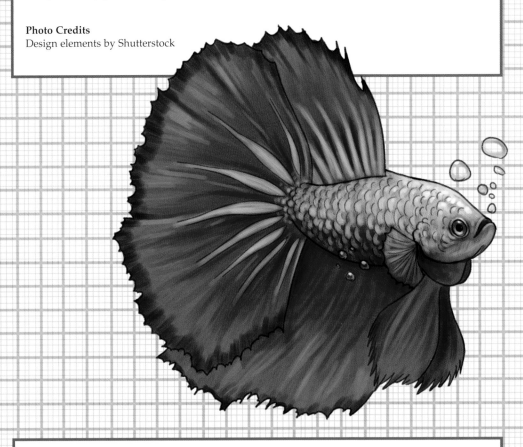

Printed in the United States of America in
North Mankato, Minnesota.
092014   008482CGS15

Table of Contents

Getting Started

From brightly colored betta fish to playful puppies, the world is full of amazing pets. Pets are fun to learn about and fun to draw too. Whether you're skilled at sketching or new to the world of drawing, you can have fun filling pages with a wide variety of pets.

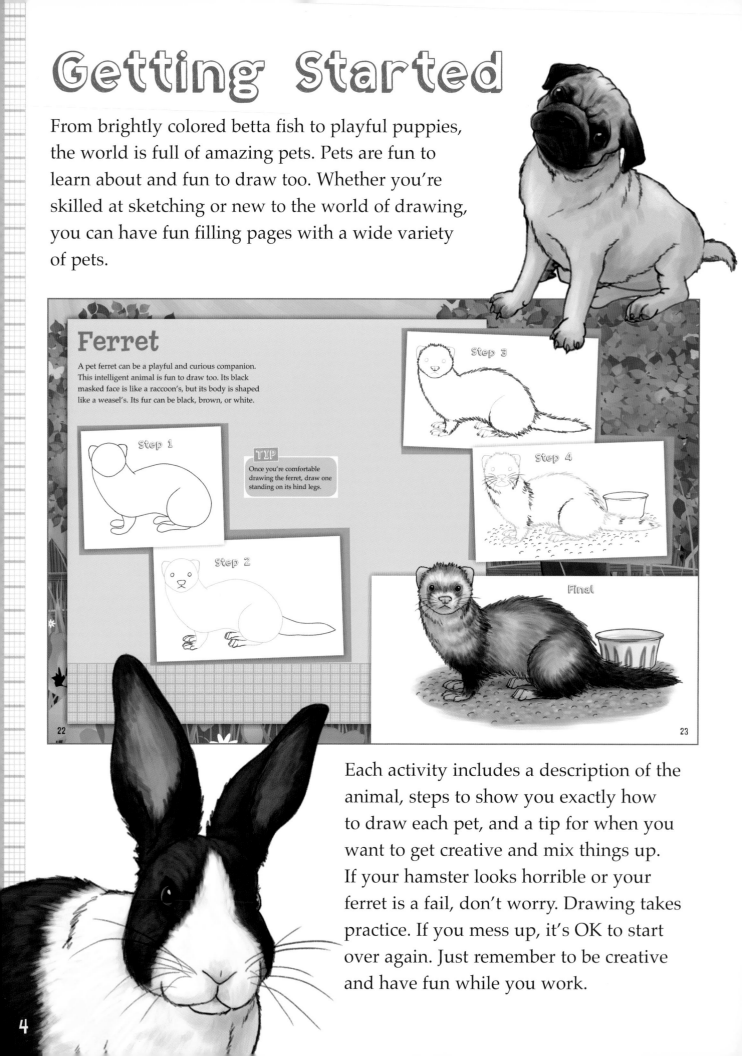

Ferret

A pet ferret can be a playful and curious companion. This intelligent animal is fun to draw too. Its black masked face is like a raccoon's, but its body is shaped like a weasel's. Its fur can be black, brown, or white.

Step 1

TIP
Once you're comfortable drawing the ferret, draw one standing on its hind legs.

Step 2

Step 3

Step 4

Final

22

23

Each activity includes a description of the animal, steps to show you exactly how to draw each pet, and a tip for when you want to get creative and mix things up. If your hamster looks horrible or your ferret is a fail, don't worry. Drawing takes practice. If you mess up, it's OK to start over again. Just remember to be creative and have fun while you work.

Tools of the Trade

Drawing is a fun and inexpensive way to express yourself and your creativity. Before you get started, be sure you have the proper tools.

Paper

Any white paper will work, but a sketchbook meant just for drawing is best.

Pencils

Any pencil will do, but many artists prefer graphite pencils made especially for drawing.

Color

A good set of colored pencils will give you many options for color. You can also try using markers or paint. Many artists enjoy outlining and filling in their work with artist pens.

Sharpener

Your pencils will be getting a lot of use, so be sure you have a sturdy sharpener. A good sharpener will give your pencil a nice, sharp point.

Eraser

Be sure to get a good eraser. Choose an eraser that won't leave smudges on your clean, white paper.

Electronics

Many great apps and programs allow you to draw on screen rather than on paper. If you want to give this medium a try, have an adult help you get started. Learn all the features and functions before you begin.

Betta Fish

Betta fish, also known as Siamese fighting fish, might be aggressive to other fish, but they are lovely to watch. These fish come in many gorgeous colors, including oranges, reds, blues, and greens. You can capture their vibrant shades best when you draw their large, flowing fins extended outward.

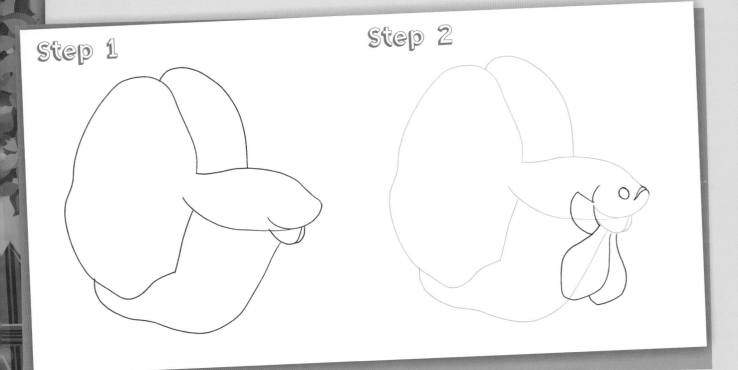

Step 1

Step 2

TIP

Try drawing a betta with its fins down at its sides. It is just as colorful and beautiful!

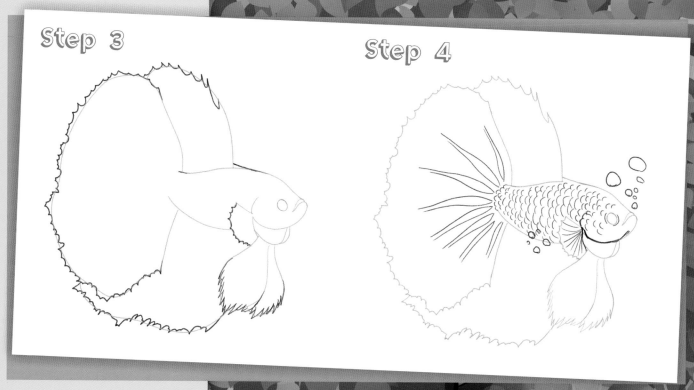

Step 3

Step 4

Final

Hamster

The cute and fluffy hamster is so small it can fit in the palm of your hand. This rodent comes in a variety of sizes and colors. Its paws look like tiny hands. Don't forget that detail when drawing this fun pet.

Step 1

Step 2

TIP

Hamsters need exercise! Draw a wheel with your hamster running inside it.

Step 3

Step 4

Final

Tree Frog

If you own a tree frog, then you know to keep it wet. But you can stay dry while drawing this amazing amphibian. Have fun as you fill in the neon green body, blue markings, red eyes, and orange feet.

Step 1

Step 2

TIP

Tree frogs love to climb! Draw your frog climbing up a tree.

Step 3

Step 4

Final

11

Parrot

The parrot is the only pet you can teach your language! Whether perched in its cage or on your shoulder, a parrot may want to chat as you sketch. Be sure to draw the beak curved and pointed. This feature helps the parrot crack open hard nuts.

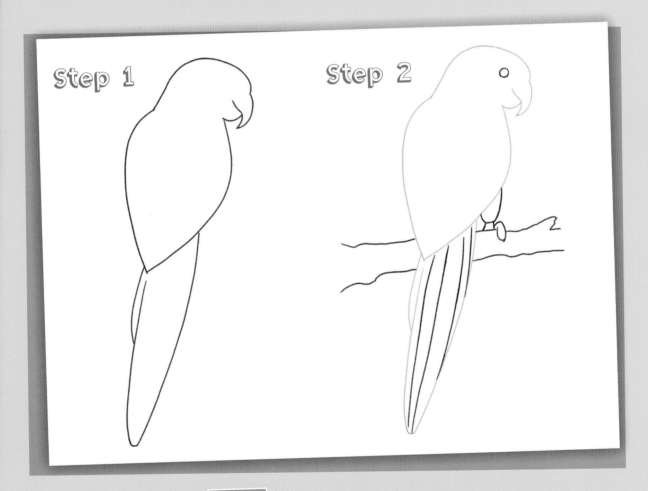

Step 1

Step 2

TIP

Parrots come in many bright colors. Experiment with different shades.

Step 3

Step 4

Final

Rabbit

A pet rabbit is cute and cuddly. Even though your paper and pencil aren't soft and furry, you can still have fun drawing this pet! Its floppy ears and cottonlike tail may be your favorite features, but don't forget the whiskers!

step 1

step 2

TIP

Pet rabbits like to hide under furniture. Can you draw a rabbit peeking out from under your bed?

Step 3

Step 4

Final

Cat

Cats are playful and mischievous creatures. They'll
scurry across the floor chasing their toys, hide in a
corner, and jump from high spaces. Then they'll curl
up next to you for a nap. Capture the amazing life of a
pet cat with this sketch.

Step 1

Step 2

TIP

Cats always land on their feet
when jumping from high spaces.
Try capturing your cat making a
smooth landing.

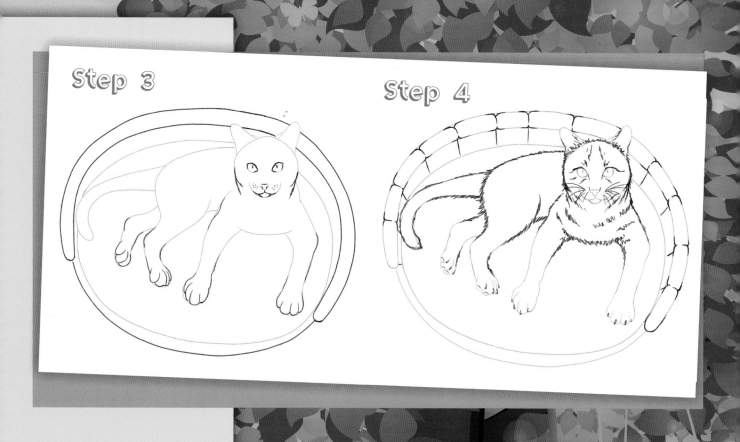

Step 3

Step 4

Final

Pug with Puppies

What's cuter than a pug? Pug puppies, of course! Sketch these dogs with their wrinkly faces, boxy bodies, and curly tails. Most pugs sport a shade of light brown fur called fawn, but they can also be black, gray, or white.

Step 1

Step 2

TIP

Draw one of your pug puppies playing fetch with a tennis ball.

Step 3

Step 4

continued on next page

Step 5

Step 6

Final

Ferret

A pet ferret can be a playful and curious companion. This intelligent animal is fun to draw too. Its black masked face is like a raccoon's, but its body is shaped like a weasel's. Its fur can be black, brown, or white.

Step 1

TIP

Once you're comfortable drawing the ferret, draw one standing on its hind legs.

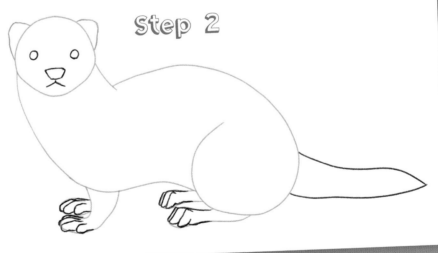

Step 2

Step 3

Step 4

Final

23

Horse

Shiny, beautiful hair growing from a long, flowing mane is just one majestic quality of the horse. A horse's personality shows through in its facial expressions. When you re-create this beautiful being on paper, be sure to catch it in its graceful gallop.

Step 1

Step 2

TIP

Once you master the horse, add a saddle and reins.

24

Step 3

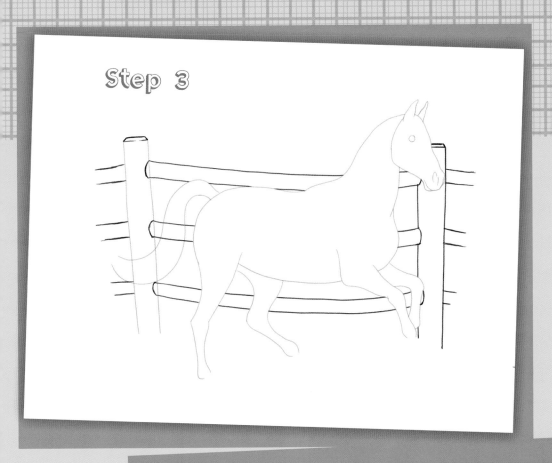

Step 4

continued on next page

Step 5

Step 6

Final

Tropical Fish Tank

Colorful fish swimming to and fro. Plants swaying back and forth. A sea star resting on the rocks. Put this beautiful scene together by drawing a tropical fish tank. Take your time sketching the details, and have fun filling in the colors.

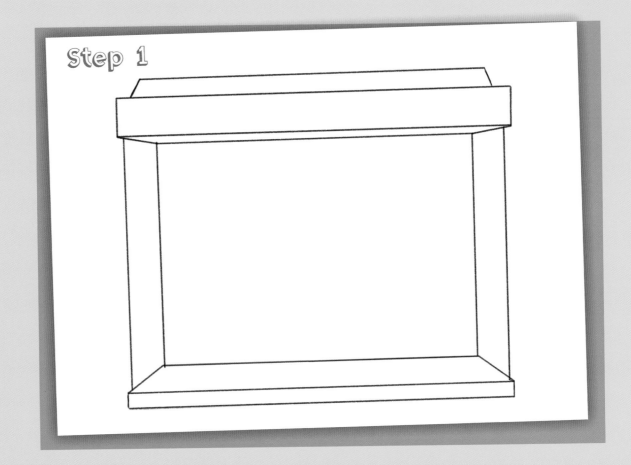

Step 1

TIP

Do you know how to draw any other fish tank creatures? Perhaps a shrimp or a little eel? Try adding these to your tank.

Step 2

Step 3

continued on next page

Step 4

Internet Sites

FactHound offers a safe, fun way to find Internet sites related to this book. All of the sites on FactHound have been researched by our staff.

Here's all you do:

Visit *www.facthound.com*

Type in this code: 9781491421345

 **Super-cool stuff!** Check out projects, games and lots more at **www.capstonekids.com**

Look for all the books in this series!